LET NOT YOUR HEART BE HARDENED

TO: MR & MRS. Kimme!
MAY GOD BLESS
you and your
Family

11/23/2022

Gene Nkazi

A True Story Written by
MUYA MONIIQUE NKAZI
AND
MR. JOE LOUIS DUSTER

Library of Congress Cataloging - in - Publication Data
Duster, Joe.
Let Not Your Heart Be Hardened / Joe Duster.
ISBN: 149299944X
ISBN-13: 9781492999447
Library of Congress Control Number: 2013919132
CreateSpace Independent Publishing Platform
North Charleston, South Carolina
Written by Muya Monique Nkazi, in Zambia the southern part of Africa
Edited & written by Joe Duster, in the United States of America
Printed & edited by CreateSpace, in the United States of America
Identity disclaimer: Names were changed to protect the identity
of people and places.
Written in American and British English.

CONTENTS

3

In Memory Of

This Book Is Dedicated in Memory of the deceased love ones that played a very important role in my life. Grandparents: Charlie & Wilner Barnett, Spencer & Hattie Mae Cole Brewer, Ellis Duster.

Parents: Joe Louis Barnett & Mary Louise Cole. Clarence Edward Barnett, Andrew James Cole Sr., Clarence James Cole, Christine Barnett Buchanan, Charlie Barnett Jr., Darrell Eric Doss, Tommy Lee Johnson, John Bennie Young, Terry Glenn Cole, Dennis Lee Cole, Mr. & Mrs. Luther Lee Duster, Mr. & Mrs. John L. Duster.

Joe Perry Beck, Santonia (Nanny) Johnson, A. Hodges, Eddie Washington Summerhill, Richella Payne, Minnie Benford, Pastor Frank Roach, Solomon (Doc) & Flora Cole, Pastor A.J. Mayes, Robert L. (Cubby) Asher.

Acknowledgements

I WOULD LIKE to thank Mr. Tim Kelley English Instructor and Chairman of The Humanities and Fine Arts Division at Northwest-Shoals Community College for his encouragement.

Special thanks go out to Northwest-Shoals Community College Librarians Mrs. Elaine C. Phillips and Mrs. Nell P. Hogan for their insightful advice. I also would like to commend Frank L. Eastland, for his accomplishment, while becoming the first African American helicopter pilot in the Tri-Cities Area. Thank you for your leadership.

Dr. Fredonia Barnett Williams you were my strength and I cannot thank you enough for your guidance throughout the most crucial times of my life. Your kindness will always be treasured. Thank You!

Debbie! You and your family gave me so much hope, and I will never forget the Brink Family. Thank You!

Pamela, Andrew Cole Jr., Leemarquette, Bernita, Barbara Tolliver, Gaye, Nettie, Betsy, Richard, Deborah, Ronald, Betty, Corey, E. Coats, S. Pendleton., D. Jordan, L. L. Whitten, C. Bohannon, M. & T. Wilson.

Dr. Billy Brewton, Pastor Curtis Russell, Jay Harding, Darryl (Skip) Tatum, Lois and Michael Evans, Michael Bradley, Dr. Robert Cummings, Terry Richter, James P. Cornell, Celesta, Vicky. Ethelene Duster, Monique R., Linda Namuchelenje Mugala Ambali!

Special thanks, goes out to my GOD sent Mother, Mrs. Nazerine Harris, and my Barnett, Beckwith, Brewer, Cole and Duster Family.

Chandelis Roshae Duster! My Dearest Daughter! I love you and thank the LORD for you. Always stand up for the LORD. "If you don't stand up for the LORD, why should the LORD stand up for you?"

There are many people in Shoals Area that were very influential; I cannot name them all. You know who you are.

THANK YOU!

1

JOE DUSTER'S *HEART raced, thudding against the walls of his body.* His head pounded fiercely while his eyes took on a momentarily glare. He could see his fingers shifting back and forth as if moving to a mellow - blues number with a taunting title called "Fear." No matter how many times he experienced it, fear never deterred him; their unsolicited meetings always felt virgin.

Incoherent voices outside the warehouse resonated with protestations and thundered like a mighty fountain. This villainous act of aggression suddenly triggered memories of his childhood. They flooded before him like a film on a projector...

Story 1

Early Childhood Years

He was four years old when he noticed the fountain and, as a curious child, advanced toward it.

That early July morning, sunny rays bathed Joe and his mother as the two walked from Washington Boulevard to the hospital. The distance wasn't far and Joe found the trip exciting. His mother was taking him to visit his grandmother.

When the Cole family had finished their visit, Mary for no apparent reason, decided to exit the hospital's outlet that lay on the west wing of the building.

In Joe's young mind, everything was fascinating, a moment of discovery. There in the central part of the grounds stood a radiant fountain and its glorious promise to quench thirsts. Joe, undaunted by the spillage, advanced to the fountain, stretching his arms, his little hands folded into a shallow hollow, but deep enough to hold water. His squeezed-together palms left a crevice between his fingers, where water was passing through. He withdrew with anticipation and brought his lips to the silvery liquid. As he opened his mouth to drink, his mother's sharp voice startled him into immediate wakefulness.

Suddenly, she lunged at him and grabbed his hand away from the fountain as if he had profaned a sacred shrine by nearing it. She was angry; Joe was perplexed to see her distress without understanding how he had offended her. She scolded with a stern demeanour, slowly enlightening Joe about where he had erred. Now he understood: Joe Duster had drunk from a fountain meant for "Whites only."

There was a fountain for blacks that Joe would have taken a drink from without causing a horrifying reaction from his mother. The fountains were marked in black and white; one read "Colored Only" in block letters and the other, "Whites Only." That was his first encounter with what he had been taught was "racism." He was no longer gullible about his surroundings. At that moment, Joe realized a sad truth about his homeland: blacks and whites lived segregated lives.

"Put your heads down now!" Uncle Doc shouted in a sotto voice, blanketing exasperation clearly threaded in his tone and the children reacting to his promptings, quickly ducking behind the car's front seat.

It was a high-performance 1956 four door sedan, three on the column. It had seen many thrills on the road. Unknown to its current occupants, the car would have to rise to the occasion and exhibit its powerful motor skills. Lives threatened with imminent danger would hinge on its speed.

As Joe squatted behind the seat, the smell of stale car shampoo rose through his nostrils, fresh air a gust just above his head. The threat was poignant enough to have raised his anxiety. Joe didn't understand why he was squatting but the look he saw in Uncle Doc's eyes had enough emphasis to keep him lying low on the car's base. He heard the sound of screeching tires, smelt the burnt rubber, and, in one motion, felt the car make a perfect 180-degree turn. It would have been an exciting joy ride if it wasn't for the quickening fear.

A deafening silence hovered. Joe and his cousins were as mute as could be, as if sworn into secrecy over illegal waste being dumped in a highly regarded city, and *now Uncle Doc had stepped on the accelerator, the kids slamming against the back seat.* When he had driven for a few minutes, his voice filled with anxiety, Uncle Doc yelled louder this time, asking if the kids were alright. When assured, he sighed deeply, exhaling in relief but clearly frustrated and livid.

Not understanding what had just transpired, Joe curiously tapped his uncle's shoulder and asked what was wrong, but when there wasn't an answer, he wisely sat back in his lone confusion. From then on, a heavy silence enveloped the car until they reached home. It was only after a few minutes, still seated in the car, that he broached the subject again.

"Did you guys see those men at the far end of West Mobile Street? The ones with the large crosses, wearing white gowns and masks?"

Rose and Junior nodded yes in unison.

"Those men were the Klan."

There was a stunned silence in the car. Each passenger was privy to his fears, thoughts eroding out of each one's mind at a slow pace. It was as if God had given a command for time to reduce its speed. Everything seemed to be moving in slow motion at that point.

With his little mind wandering, Joe, although equally as stunned as the others, having been acquainted with the sudden, startling emotion of fear was five years old when this happened. It was barely months after the incident at the fountain with his mother. What Uncle Doc had added was merely the cherry topping by giving the children firm safety advice: "*Keep away from the Klan and if seen by them, run.*"

The car seat that Joe was sitting on suddenly towered above him. Feeling feverish, he understood that he had to steer clear from the men in white apparel and from fountains marked "Whites Only" or risk a stern scolding and a possibility of death.

After the short lecture, Uncle Doc placed his arms on the steering wheel and rested his head, obviously wishing that he'd stayed at the house with Aunt Flo. Joe gazed out and internalized the scenery, thinking, with tears threatening, *'What if the sedan had resisted movement...what if?'*

The shivers of fear persisted...

Born on February 1, 1957, Joe lived with his grandmother and siblings in Florence, Alabama. Through his eyes, the world was a community in which family was replicated in splinter groups. Benevolence in acts of sharing and caring for the elderly should have been the norm in the vast community. But the world he desired to see lay at bay as the truth kept dawning that kindness, even though sought after, wouldn't avail itself to his whim.

At eight years of age, Joe decided to pragmatically do something to defy the inertia around him. He began visiting the sick and elderly, did mundane jobs, and often volunteered to run errands that other children would have had to be forced to do. He found in this a great deal of satisfaction deep within his soul. At only eight years old, there was a resonance in Joe that those who knew him, and had been receptive of his heart's giving, could not forget. This young boy knew if anyone could stand and make a difference, he was going to be the one. These acts of love, menial as they may have seemed to other people, became a passion and a form of entertainment for Joe. For when other children were at play, he felt the need to make a senile old man cheer up at his appearance; a few hours of compassion, a minute of love, changed many sulks into joyful banter.

Perhaps this kind of affection was coming from a heart that was seeking the love and care not gotten from its mother. His acts of kindness could have been a reflection of his need to be cuddled by the woman who had birthed him.

It was a chilly Monday morning and, at seven months pregnant, Mary Louise knew her baby's time to arrive was not rightfully due. But the labor pains she had started experiencing reassured her constantly that the baby's journey in the birth canal had begun. Local medical facilities were not equipped to handle premature delivery and Mary knew her baby's life was hanging on by a thread. She was certain its passage would be most difficult and its death assured.

Self-induced labor was not common in the 1950s and many who had the courage and money to afford midwives never came back to tell of the horror. Mary Louise was fifteen years old at the time. Her mother was horrified by the act of trying to cut short an innocent life.

Hattie Mae was injured by her daughter's cold demeanour, revulsion building up as nausea as she took to caring for the child immediately after it was born.

Mary Louise had given birth to a baby boy, whom she christened Joe Louis Duster, adopting her father's surname.

The little child weighed just three pounds at birth and, within a week, was down to two. Life seemed to be fading and this worried his grandmother. His mother, near death herself, could not take on the responsibility of breastfeeding her young, so Grandma became the twenty-four-hour caregiver.

The incubator had an effect on baby Joe. Whenever darkness would fall, he would cry in desperation and Hattie Mae would hold him in her loving arms as if she had birthed him herself. The task of raising a new child had been bestowed upon her. She was appointed by God to raise this child as her very own. She would teach him Christian values and make him a fearless man.

Her fear of losing the baby subsided as the boy seemed to stave off what she felt sure was ensuing death, guised as a mere malady due to premature arrival.

Joe had unction about him. His eyes glowed with promise. As he grew, giving his grandmother few troubles, she took full responsibility for the child and saw to his needs as a God-fearing mother would. Mary's brothers, Sonny and Clarence, always said that the Almighty had given Joe a unique gift.

He began to see and understand things of nature, often living without certain luxuries; this lad, at a very young age, experienced what it was to be poor. He had lived a life fused with both joy and pain. In his eyes, growing up without both parents but raised by his grandparents presented him a chance to succeed, learn from their values, and be loved as their own child. However, he knew there was no amount of substitution that could adequately suffice for his birth parents' love. During the summer, Joe's cousins the Beckwith and Whitten families would come down from Chicago and it somehow would ease the pain.

Grandpa Spencer was a very humble man who spent most of his time on the road. He worked as a truck driver for a local company, delivering tires throughout the United States. Hattie Mae Cole Brewer was left to fend for the children, often accepting the role of being both husband and wife. She had the strength of many warriors and championed her home the best way that she could. The children revered her much and, to Joe, the squalid surroundings in which his family lived never acted as a deterrent. There was so much inadequacy in his life that the very life he lived felt as if it were borrowed.

His cousin Cornell often said that Joe was different. What he saw in him was the determination to serve the world and make a difference by sharing and giving. Although what he had in his hands was nothing, he devoted his gifts of love into time.

As time would lapse and Grandpa's trips home were well overdue, there would always be an air of expectancy within the family. Hattie Mae would take on the semblance of a youthful girl, tying her hair into coils of beauty, oiling her lips with petroleum jelly. The children, ever hopeful, would know that his arrival would mean a good meal and much laughter. Everyone missed Grandpa Spencer.

Joe loved trucks, especially large ones—always dreaming of driving, visualizing himself being behind the steering wheel. Grandpa Spencer was truly his idol.

Joe had been seated in the room that served as the living quarters. The house was a five-room structure that accommodated seven family members. Now, his mind meandering, thinking about nothing in particular, he heard the tapping of shoes on the creaking floor of the boarded porch. It was a familiar sound, a pleasant one; it was Grandpa's arrival.

Instead of dashing to give him a hug, the boy waited, seated on the edge of the chair, fearing to be disappointed in a moment of expectation. The tapping grew louder and the boy's anticipation heightened. When he saw the domineering presence of his grandfather, he dashed to embrace him wholeheartedly.

After Grandpa was settled, he called the children and slowly began to present them with gifts. It was with much expectation that Joe sat waiting, wondering what gift would be his to keep. Grandpa reached into the gray bag that he always carried, looking straight in the boy's eyes as if trying to read for gratitude, and extracted a toy. It was a shiny red fire engine. The boy, wide-eyed with joy, stood up and received the gift with deep gratitude. He hugged his grandpa and settled in bed for reflection.

He marvelled at the beauty of the truck, instantly falling in love with it, turning it upside down for inspective admiration. Joe slept with the fire truck that fateful night.

Story 2

First Experience of Puppy Love

The red fire engine became his favorite toy among his repertoire, and he carried it at all times. He felt the bravery that made fire-fighters complete, sacrificing their own lives and safety for others, descend upon him. It was some form of spiritual anointing. He felt a zeal that no amount of water would quench and, at eight years of age, Joe nurtured an interest in fire fighting.

He was keen to visit the local fire department but his idea was a mere dream; he knew that black people were not allowed at the station. He understood that the black man was perceived to be afraid of heights and fire fighting. This dented the boy's morale. But the demeaning thoughts were surmountable to many.

In the late '60s and early '70s, his Uncle Sam in Oakland, California, and Cousin William in Detroit, Michigan, were firefighters whom Joe admired. The men gave him the initiative to keep on pushing. Apart from serving the community with chores and errands, he was going to ensure that fire didn't singe any of his neighbour's homes, visualizing this with only a fire suit, a safety cap, and a water hose. He had not told anyone about his aspirations but kept looking for a chance to share it with his grandmother.

Joe knew that the shared acts of love displayed by her would welcome his decision to serve in spite of the perilous nature of the job. She was fearless as a woman, and no amount of fire would have destroyed her will power. He patiently waited for the proper time to present himself to her.

As Duster grew older, observing a myriad of problems among the black community, the poverty that his sister, Pamela, and brother, Andrew, had been encumbered with, he also noticed a very shy girl. Amelia Williams was her name. She had long black hair and a beautiful, round face. The young boy wasn't sure if she knew that he existed. But Joe was now determined to make her his own.

It was his first experience of puppy love, and she was the girl of his dreams. Things naturally fell into place, her reception quickly thwarting away his fears of competition from the throng of admirers among his classmates. He began slowly visiting the Williams' home, having been adored by Amelia's parents. It could have been his gentle demeanour, his soft-spoken tone that swept her off her feet. He didn't care about reasons and reasoning—only that she agreed to be his girlfriend and stood true to the expectation of the primary relationship, which was letter-writing and very rare, stolen, special instances of holding hands.

She left town eventually, leaving Joe with a broken heart to nurse.

But Amelia's soft response to his offer of friendship had carbon-copied the affection he had been lacking from his birth mother. They had shared an innocent love that had no sexual connotation about it, but the warmth and peace between them signified for him a hopeful future of finding a wife who would shower him with love.

Story 3

A Firehouse Tour

There was an announcement made at the local Elementary School stating that the children were going on a field trip that Friday. It was with much exhilaration that Joe received the news because they were going to be visiting the local fire station. The children were enthused by the promise of the visit, but for Joe it was a significant time of his young life.

The visit was uproar. The children had a rare educational tour and Joe took it all in with admiration, consuming every detail. He noticed the unique helmets and was immediately intrigued by the men sliding down the fire pole. The shiny red trucks stood out like no others; he was overwhelmed.

Still, it was not lost on him that his desire to serve in that building was limited to a sheer peek through the window, and would remain so. He went home uplifted, albeit discouraged that his dream to be a fireman would remain but a dream.

Story 4

Summer of 1974

Years had lapsed since the school trip to the station, and the fire that had keenly flickered within him, burning to be a fireman, had since dwindled to a feeble flame.

One Saturday afternoon, he sat watching the television series "Faith" with his cousins Robert and Andre. They were on vacation, visiting their aunt Hattie Mae, during the summer of 1974.

Their eyes affixed on the bulky but reliable TV set as "Faith" unfolded, much to their dismay. It was about a black fireman who was subjected to extreme racial prejudice within an all-white organization. The program shocked and hurt him so that tears welled in his eyes. His cousins were not subjected to such treatment in the city of Chicago.

Detailed truth was now unravelling, truth of how hateful and segregated life was among blacks and whites, truth of how it was difficult for the black man to ascend to the echelons of power at any level in society. Truth glared and something fueled to a boiling point within. Profoundly enraged, wroth at the raw display of hatred, Joe found a determination to act at that significant point, and he firmly fortified his decision to dance with the flames in the arena.

"Faith "became the final stamp that sealed his fate. That was the catalyst that strengthened his desire, as an unbeatable giant leaped within him, arising with triumph. He was only seventeen years old.

2

Story 5

Growing up on Fayette Street

As he grew up, he accepted the knowledge that there were obstacles placed in everyone's life, dreams, and aspirations. To him, the impediments came surnamed as Mr. Poverty, Mr. Injustice, Mr. Hurt.

He and his childhood neighbours calling themselves "The Fayette Street Boys," came up with an idea of raising money for their school needs. The young teenagers began doing yard work and washing cars in the community at a miserly fee. Friend Garner, a very nice lady who lived on the next street, was inspiring. She encouraged them to do what was right. It made all the difference in the world to them.

There was also a lady who taught Bible school across the street. She had a generous heart and was compassionate to the children in the community as well. She would give the children Bible verses, Easter speeches, and Christian books to read, then reward them afterwards. The children called her Miss Minnie. He would live on to remember the impact of her benevolence and the difference it made.

He felt blessed to have had two grandmothers. They were his inspiration and mainly his source of comfort. Granny, Mrs. Barnett, had a very soothing voice. There was something therapeutic about it that surmounted the emotional absence at hand. To her, family was a cardinal structure that was to be valued and respected.

Joe had taken the privilege to share with them his dreams of becoming a fireman and they both said that he could be anything, that he wanted to be, if only he believed.

Joe understood that his family was poor but couldn't fathom the squalid surroundings that he was raised in. There was so much squalor in the home, he felt sometimes as if the place made his dreams small. The thought of becoming a fireman was a mockery considering the state of his present surroundings.

One evening, while he was playing with his favourite toy, his mother appeared and stood in front of him. The child, stooped to the ground, pushing his truck, recognized the feet he was staring at as his mother's; he immediately sat up and looked at her face to face.

"I hear you want to become a fireman?" She asked. Joe nodded excitedly and was about to begin his narrative on how he was going to save many lives when she interrupted him in mid-sentence, saying, "*You will never be anything in life. Your life will not amount to nothing,*" *and she walked off.*

Joe was left embroiled in hurt and confusion. He was left asking himself why she always had an angry disposition toward him, why it was that she always stood in opposition to his dreams. Something irreparable broke in Joe's heart that day; it was a loss of confidence in his mother. A son's loving awe of his mother was now corroded with malice.

Joe's eyes swelled with silvery tears and, as they trickled down his cheeks, he took the red fire truck and began pushing it to and fro, losing consciousness of reality. He was lost to the motion of the wheels he pushed.

The sound of wheels screeching on the floor increased and Joe's ears deafened into the sound, shutting off all manner of thought and vision, losing coherence. *The sound took him to a place unlike any other.* Like butter being churned, he thought constantly, *'I am going to make it...I am going to make it...I am going to make it..."*

The truth was laid bare. Even though it was always there glaring back at him, Joe would choose to see the best in his mother's cruelty. He always tried to win her affection by doing what he surmised would please her, but his efforts were inadequate to woo her obstinate heart. There was no quid pro quo between the two; their relationship was he gave and she took and never gave back, like the grave that never got satisfied. She was placid toward his mollifications, adamant to not reciprocate affectionately. He wondered often where he had wronged her. How a mother could despise a son she had carried in her womb for months...

He never stopped wondering.

Story 6

Teenage Years

Joe had reached puberty and, as a promising young man, began following in the footsteps of his uncles, Harry, Sam, Clarence, James and Charlie Jr., who were great athletes. They set the trend and he began seeing life for what it was. His Cole cousins, Larry, Terry and Lonnie served as a blueprint in life as well.

While attending a local JR. High School, Joe met Samantha Ward. *She stood tall and beautiful, and Joe knew she was the one.* She was very mild-mannered and adequately well-bred.

She was the one who would fill the hole of loneliness he had felt from childhood. It was the limbo of nothingness where the crowd in the home did not suffice for his need to be loved. She was the prettiest thing he had ever laid eyes on and there he made a decision secretly that he, Joe Duster, would marry Samantha and spend the rest of his life with her.

The two dated for several years, their relationship soaring to greater heights, love blossoming as spring's early produce.

He found another passion. It was the love of basketball that he used to frustrate his boredom and keep him away from mischief. Joe spent most of his time away from home in Clover Heights, with the Williams and Wilkinson families. They all were very close friends.

For some strange reason, he had been harbouring a desire to feel Samantha's lips against his. He wasn't sure how to broach the subject and was encumbered with mixed feelings. Because of her conservative manner, he now felt as if she would reject him and the foresight simply paralyzed him.

One hot summer day, as Joe was leaving the gym, he approached Samantha while she was on her way home from volleyball practice. She had a glow about her that day that softened the hardest part of him. He wanted her. He just had to kiss her and, as she was talking, unaware of him approaching, his lips met hers in a fumbled attempt for a perfect kiss. Joe, nervous, not touching her, opened his eyes to see the impact of his mischief and was relieved to notice that she had not pulled back. Her eyes were firmly shut against the ambient sound and activities. He read that as an invitation for furthered romance so, without a waste of time; he pulled himself together and placed his lips on hers. She parted hers in submission and Joe proceeded, with immature bravado, to smooch Samantha out of all her strength.

The withdrawal left Joe feeling a weakening in his limbs. The kiss lasted for a minor five seconds, but for him it felt like ETERNITY.

He walked home with butterflies in his stomach. He kept reminiscing about the kiss, loving the feeling, the memory evoked in him. Thinking to himself, 'If this is love, I certainly want more of it.'

As he entered the Barnett home, Joe noticed Mr. Barnett, who was his biological dad's father, working in the garden. Granddaddy had just returned from the co-op and because he loved gardening, Mr. Barnett would spend most of his time outside watering plants and picking vegetables.

Joe walked up to his granddad and asked him if he could help out. Usually when gardening, his granddad would have to ask him if he was available. But being mesmerized by the enormity of that first kiss, it changed the young man's way of thinking. *Mr. Barnett began by showing him how to plant onions and then proceeded advising him on how to live as a real man. He taught him that a man would arise early and would take responsibility for his family. He was taught to stand up for what was right and have good work ethics. He taught him that honesty should be upheld in all traits of life.*

Joe learned during these intimate times that to be a real, honourable man was to be entwined with prayer. As a young man, he knew about God's everlasting power and learned how to pray.

It was as if Granddad was filling in for his son's failure to raise a young man. He gave him his all, imparting his heart's very core to ensure a man was made. Joe grew tall and wiser by the day and began to realize that his dad loved him in spite of his faults, and showed love in a peculiar way. *Joe Louis Barnett was his guardian.*

Story 7

High School and the Military

There was a soft-spoken man in the neighbourhood that everyone called Mr. Clark, who was a mentor to many kids in the town. Mr. Johnny Clark and his wife was a very cordial couple. Joe admired the way Mr. Clark loved his wife, how she, too, responded to his whims, especially the way the two simply managed their lives.

One day he decided to approach Johnny and ask him for a job. Being a teenager, Joe realized that growing up came with demands. Mr. Clark was kind enough to accept him as one of his own and allowed odd jobs to surface.

It wasn't long before Joe realized that Mr. Clark was a man with great attributes, an honourable man, true to his word. Joe felt that he was an inspiration to him.

There was an understanding between the two of them, matters shared only between a father and a son. The two grew fond of each other, with Mr. Clark as Joe's mentor in all aspects of life. Therefore, Joe worked hard during high school, juggling time between study and part-time work.

As Joe was retiring from teen life, a handsome man had emerged, tall and brave. That was the façade he allowed the world to see. Beneath the veneer, he was a man fraught with fear. It was especially the fear to fail that emerged stronger than the other ones. He suspected it was because his mother kept reminding him that he would never make it in life. Never the less, he soldiered on tenaciously.

It was no surprise, therefore, when Joe Duster told his family that he, O'Bryan, and Jerome had enrolled in the Navy. The usual pessimists rose with a negative vibe but he knew that he was to serve.

In August, after graduating from High School, Duster left for military training. Leaving home was a break from the negative and needful surroundings. It was a breath of fresh air because he was tired of smelling the *bootleg whiskey his grandmother sold to make ends meet.* Joe had learned to perceive whiskey as an evil necessity because it was the source of income for the family. The poverty, the whiskey, his mother's negative talk was much persuasion for him to work hard and leave the area. His goal was to be an honourable man that loved and cared for others.

He was going to get married and love his family. These were the motivations that wheeled him out of Alabama into Orlando, Florida, to boot camp.

When their training was completed, the three were sent to San Diego, California. While attending the Naval School of Health and Science, months had passed and Joe was enjoying it, but much to his chagrin, a friend of his was killed during an incident at Balboa Park. With this tragic incident and due to an injury, Joe received orders and was sent to the East Coast. As time slowly passed, he received an honourable discharge. Joe was proud to have served his country.

He had a strong inclination, surprisingly, that it was in his hometown where destiny was calling.

Alabama received Joe with fascination, the primary feeling being that of respect for him having ventured out and braved California, but then melancholy later settled a heavy dust of apprehension because he had returned anyway. For Joe, coming back home was very significant and revealing. It became the matrix of a myriad of events unfolding.

Since he had received an honourable discharge, he had no reason to feel abased but was pining to see Samantha. During his first few months home, extremely depressed. A strange incident with a box cutter in a suicide attempt failed. Alcohol and cannabis also reared their ugly heads.

Weeks later, he announced his presence at Samantha's parents' house one warm evening. The scene was serene and calmness had settled. In the distance, birds chirped from an aerial view.

Samantha looked lovelier than before. Her eyes shone and deep within them he saw something peculiar that he decided was love for him, not tethered, intoning silently within. Those eyes were the windows to the soul.

Through them he was sure he had just violated the soul's privacy. Her silky skin shone against the retiring sun and the planes of her cheeks were so smooth Joe couldn't wait to have his cheek against hers in an affectionate and loving embrace. They took a walk hand in hand. When they had exhausted their lovers' small talk, Samantha indicated that she had something to say.

She said, "Joe, I know that you and I have come a long way." Joe nodded emphatically. She then proceeded to tell him that she was leaving the area for college. The news rammed into him with a shock.

"Well," Samantha went on, "I will return."

His initial reaction was a mélange. It was a mixture of well-wishing joy and eroding fear. The joy was his expression of generosity. *He loved Samantha and because education was important to Joe, he wanted his woman to be equally scholarly empowered.* He had seen her young and beautiful, from a tender age, and had celebrated her youthfulness, and now she was bloomed into a superb young woman. She had increasingly become a woman with great promise. It was a promise to make him a great wife. The joy translated into the heroine.

The joy had a nemesis: the fear. The gnawing fear was energizing his tension, portraying taunting pictures of her being loved by another man, pictures that rendered him temporarily hopeless. Fear was emerging villainous and mightier than the heroine.

Samantha had a sensitive spirit, calm as a spring, but wiser than many women Joe had met in his life.

When she noticed that Joe wasn't amused at the idea of being left behind, she turned to placate him, assuring him that they would survive the distance apart. Joe felt an alien knocking in his peripheral senses and it came with a force rare and frightening. He had a sinking feeling suddenly in his belly but decided that Samantha would remain his, raising her word of promise as the standard of authority that stood as the earnest reflection of her truest truths. She never lied, so he knew he could count on her word.

A brooding, melancholy mood had descended and settled like dust on the two love birds. His return home was the sign for him to strengthen his love with the love of his life. He had made his decision to declare his intention to marry her. On the threshold of proposing, he was given an impression that things had surely fallen apart. The two parted on a promise to meet again but the rendezvous was left unoccupied by them, other lovers meeting there a futile sham.

Another place, another time, one year later during spring break they met again, both masquerading as the happy couple, and he who always looked to obtain good even in worst-case scenarios tried to cajole her into a love frenzy by planting a kiss on her jaw, hoping that by doing so the fear that was warning, lurking, in the thickets of disappointment would take a bow of shame and leave. To an inexperienced eye, Joe would have looked like a desperate, inconsiderate lover, but there was a very poignant, familiar feeling of hurt approaching. Fear. She thwarted his unbridled passions by standing up. He knew at that point for sure that Samantha standing tall above him, her beauty taunting and unrelenting, had joined forces with those who couldn't care less if he was hurt, waving proverbial hands of departure and therefore doing what was common to Joe: breaking his heart.

He stood up from the bench they'd been sitting on, dusted his rear of imaginary feathers, and took her back home.

His lone walk back home brought about many memories; he saw them all bare and glaring: moments of rejection, shame, and lack of love. A part of him that in the past had been coarse, the part that had been covered by Samantha's warmth and love, now lay exposed and threatened because she had transformed her pure love into a monstrous mockery, making it the very instrument for hurting him. She had carried with her the protective covering that had shielded him from the pain he was used to and now, open to self-scrutiny, he allowed the past emotions to flow.

Although these were emotional memories he would have rather buried, they obstinately arose with a fury of the unforgiving. There was something amiss in her that he couldn't really pinpoint, but he knew that it was a sign of the end from her attitude.

Story 8

The Final Verdict

Although the news came with a blow, time had assuaged the bitter, destructive effect it could have had on him, should he have not profiled Samantha's despondency as a prognosis of those who hurt others, those whose words were like careless nails spat out through a gun, maiming many, and hearts disintegrating. Joe knew that sometimes the pieces could be picked up for remoulding but, many times, with a ferocious preparedness, the heart never really got fixed.

He looked hard at Samantha's sister as she spoke, weighing her word for word. A few months had passed, she had come to announce the final verdict, and it was to the effect that Samantha would not be returning to Alabama. Samantha felt that Joe would not be successful in accomplishing his dream to become a fireman. She had consequently found another man to love.

Joe was incapable of fighting for her. But the love needed to have come naturally, as a mother stretches her limitless love to her young. So with that transitory word from his lover, he ceded to her demands and later looked askance at the sister as she took the match of victory, leaving.

So much pain, too much betrayal, endless loves, and broken promises seemed to be the premise upon which Joe's life was made. His pain was somewhat eased that day by his relatives Brenda and Jean, the rare females that he learned to confide in.

Story 9

Naval Training

Joe received his fire fighting and damage control training in the Navy. This was the first time he had entered a burning building. As he and the rookie recruits entered the structure, he had an eerie feeling at first, but slowly began to unwind because of the reassurance of their instructor. The men had been given their first introduction to fire fighting.

The fire rose above and around the recruits like demonic forces on the attack. Their instruction was to quench the fire using a hose and a nozzle. The raging flames stood unabated with the little experience the trainees had. Joe was filled with excitement and the thought of death presented its lingering presence, making him sweat and pant in the protective gear. He was struggling to acclimatize in the suit and surrounding inferno, when he remembered that they had been told to pretend that the building was a ship. He could feel an iota of courage seeping into him and, with that, took further steps inside.

His return and subsequent loss of his lover gave Joe fortitude in pursuing fire fighting as a career. He had gotten his training, was not gullible about the reality of racism in Alabama, and so the thought of pursuing other jobs had crossed his mind, but still there was the earnest urge in his heart to work as a fire-fighter.

Joe's keen interest, and his mind made up, was the persuasion he needed to apply for a fireman's position at City Hall. He would read the newspaper daily, and to his surprise notice that applications for fire-fighters were being taken. Duster quickly applied.

It wasn't shocking when he got no response for two agonizing years. For an eager young man whose life was stooped in struggle; Joe perceived the lack of response just as one of those hurdles he had to jump. For the next three years following, Joe confronted the roster that was placed in City Hall, checking for his name, hoping he'd been appointed. The battle had begun between hope and failure. He was once again face to face with rejection; it bruised him but never daunted him enough to shatter his dream.

Five years had elapsed and Joe kept waiting...

Story 10

Breaking the Ice

On September 21, 1981, Joe Duster received a call from City Hall. The fire chief summoned the young man to appear at the administrative building downtown. When Duster arrived, the chief sat him down in his office, politely asking, "Are you sure that you want this job?" Joe replied, in a very expedient voice, "Yes, I do."

Out of concern, the fire chief replied, "This is a giant step for you and me; these are some trying times. This is not like an ordinary eight-hour job. You will be living at the firehouse with other men who are all white. This will be your permanent house, away from home; living as family with one life depending on the other. There are three shifts, twenty-four hours on and forty-eight hours off. *You will be assigned to No. 1 Fire Station, shift number one. Congratulations and welcome aboard. Joe, you have broken the color barrier as being the first black fireman in this city.*"

A few hours later, Joe Louis Duster was sworn in to uphold his duty as a fireman. As Duster and the highly decorated fire chief were exiting the room, the chief extended his hand and kindly said, *"Today, history has been made in the State of Alabama."* Joe smiled and said in a very soft tone, *"This is truly the will of God."*

It took five years for this day to come. This was Joe's first morning on shift and it was the standard procedure in the fire service that rookies be taken around to each station to acquaint themselves with their fellow firemen. His first stop was headquarters, No. 1 Fire Station.

Day One:
Joe, his confidence escalating, not believing the day of reckoning had finally dawned, walked with a gait of one whose years had been stooped in skepticism and blatant pessimism and

now knew a gush of assurance had rested upon him. He felt high self-esteem. Expectancy, requited with positive response, soared.

He had grown into a six-foot- tall man, sky scraping many, but his heart was still a meek-spirited gem.

As the two men entered the living quarters, a middle-aged man, along with the battalion chief, was leading the way. Joe felt the malicious glare of the white men in the building but nonetheless wasn't deterred. With the look of a timid newcomer, his eyes swept through the building with a photographic glance that gathered in memory people, furniture, single-colour walls, and the sound of feet, there and anon, reverberating into a song.

Joe knew that the department was an all-white cloister and the black man, deviously coined the Negro, had no room for work or frivolity there.

It didn't matter to him, at that graduate stage with racial discrimination, what color skin a human was encased in or how much indifference and hatred he was bequeathed with, because he was different. He figured if he had a heart and the color of his blood remained red, like all races, then it was vanity and lack of understanding that made men hate on the basis of skin color. Love or hatred was a choice. Joe knew he was called to serve, to love, and to lay his own life down to save lives.

Besides, all his life he had been an avid student of the art of hatred and racial segregation, and had been used as the very tool for school illustrations, later displayed for a jest or a jeer by a crowd. He was a black man in the land of the fair-skinned. He understood their fears and so could now stomach the fact that no malignity could exert enough force upon him to faze him. He was geared up and apt for anything. He had been preparing for this moment since the day he pushed the toy truck to and fro.

The battalion chief slowly opened a door that led them into a room thronged with a dozen or more white men. The entrance of the two men drew their attention. With forewarned eyes, Duster quickly observed the room; his bright eyes carefully examined each face and read the men as he stepped in. It was very quiet and one could automatically hear a pin drop. A foreboding air quickly swept through the room and those whose mouths rent into smiles quickly withdrew them, hiding enamel. Eyes that had a gentle disposition now took on a hard and violent look.

He felt their fear, acknowledged it for what it was, but bravery wasn't near to soothe him as a coach placates a beaten soldier returning into the ring. *'I don't dare show my emotions,'* he thought, his eyes fixed just a little above the head of the tallest man standing. The chief proceeded to introduce him to the men and Joe allowed his eyes to linger below just for a few seconds. A few "hellos" ascended, startling him. He was as calm as a lamb. There was no registry of a twitch or facial expression to betray his inner, discreet petrifaction. He responded with a kind and gentle "hello." Those whose silence was a clear illustration of how much they loathed him because of his dark color stared on with deathly intent.

There was an awkward chill in the room and then one of the men spoke up, breaking it. He called, and Joe quickly assumed the man was about to break the ice by offering a hand of friendship. But he was much disappointed. The act of civility wasn't reciprocated and comprehension descended. There was a need for him to exercise some patience there.

Silence engulfed the atmosphere. Then the man openly said, *"Sit down and let me tell you a nigger joke."* He furthered his mockery by beckoning him to sit on one of the two pieces of furniture in the room. Joe walked to the bench as he was bade, looking into the dry, sunken eyes of the man. He was a giant, his monstrous height threatening and intimidating by itself.

Joe had to master much restraint to keep him from lashing back with unequalled verbal rivalry. He was slightly tempted but he knew he was outnumbered and he didn't want to give the man the satisfaction. *"One's emotions are manipulated by that which affects him," he recalled his grandfather saying to him.* He swallowed hard. He didn't like confrontations but stood up for himself when he felt his life was in grave danger.

The man spoke with deliberate slowness. Every word was delivered with intention to demean and lacerate. The words left Joe with an insipid, stale aftertaste. Every word was designed and thrown to totally rend and maim veins and muscle that held his heart together. When it was indicative enough that he had finished his slanderous and barraging joke, Joe asked him, *"Are you done?" The man* pompously said, "Yes," then Joe stood and left the room with his head erect. His step was calculated, his breathing schooled; he felt a heavy burden offloaded from his chest as soon as he left the room.

He left the building feeling as hurt as one who had never been ostracized before. He was nervous, but his pulse was stable, beating with a hard thud against his chest. He was struck with much surprise that day because he thought he was immune to hurt that was based on racism. As always, he consumed the debasing remarks with dignity. He wasn't going to quit because a fearful man had demonstrated his fear, hoping it appeared as strength, Joe decided.

The next place he was then taken to was the bay area, where the fire engines were housed. The sun had gathered its entire splendour and was returning to its secret lair before the moon appeared. It was soon to be dark.

Out of curiosity, he went to the window to observe the vicinity and surroundings. There wasn't much activity around except in a distance.

Joe noticed a small gathering of men constructing a wooden figure. He walked away from the window, minding his own.

A few hours had lapsed and curiosity drew him back to the window. Across the street from the station, *Joe could see the figure being positioned.* He rapidly understood what it was the gathered crowd had been building.

The cross they had made was as tall as a telephone pole, and as his eyes swept it, *he could see that the men dressed in white were the Klan marching around it.* Their chanting and shouts rose in defiance of the new black skin in the fire department. The secret was laid bare. Joe wasn't wanted.

He felt weak in his whole body and a peculiar sadness engulfed him. He was saddened because he saw how earnest the men were in their cause, which was to discredit black men in America. Such enthusiasm and united hatred shattered his understanding and ushered in his bitter childhood rivalry. It stood taunting, threatening, and brandishing its toothless jaw in its efforts to inebriate Joe with its *Fear.*

This was his first day at work and everything he had achieved thus far stood on the brink of failure. His mother's words flashed in his mind: *"You'll never make it in life!"*

The fear ridiculed his strength to nothingness. It was the battalion chief's voice urging him to move away from the window that persuaded him to safety. The chief was clearly fearful, his facial crease lines highlighted, showing them more. He seemed worried for Joe and as they together escaped the jaws of hatred, he knew that he had found a friend and brother in the battalion chief.

Story 11

First Tragedy

Suddenly the alert tone was activated, an errant voice began to speak over the intercom, and everyone who had been busy quickly discarded whatever activity they had been engaged in. Two men rushed to the fire engine, and Joe was one of them. He had been assigned to an attack/rescue apparatus.

Joe was nervous and excited. He was placing an imprint of himself on the canvas of his dreams. It was his first emergency call.

The accident was on *an old county road,* and as they were en route, Joe could feel the tension of the engine; accompanied by his colleagues, it seemed as if the vehicle were airborne. A drop of sweat trickled on his left rib cage while, a few minutes later, sweat dots had spread to his forehead. He wiped them off with the back of his hand.

When the men arrived on the scene, sitting sideways in a ditch was a fairly new vehicle badly rammed into a tree. The fender and hood were crushed beyond repair, pushed back into the wind-shield; metal was folded and shards of glass were thrown across the road in the tall grass. The chassis was visibly disengaged from the body. It was raining, cold, pitch-black, dark, and foggy, and onlookers had gathered, watching with awesome trepidation.

Joe disembarked from the truck with intrepid, agile grace, his youthful strength propelling him to run faster than his co-worker. When he reached the car wreck, his excitement shrunk into fear.

There was a momentary restriction of time and coherence. He panicked inwardly. He felt a reckoning of might within, the dream and reality contending. It was the driver of the fire truck who had startled him back to reality.

Both fireman put their hands on the metal wreck and began to examine for signs of survivors. The driver squatted and made a gesture with sign language that there were three victims, two men and a woman, who was severely injured.

The two men performed arduous manoeuvres, pulling metal, reciprocating in giving instructions, and moments of resolute attentiveness became the order of the moment. The Jaws of Life stretched to its limit.

The closer they got to the victims, the more intense the situation became. Time became a major factor and the firemen had to work fast.

She lay on the passenger side, her neck craned in a deadly position; her legs and arms were angled unusually. She was fading in and out; seconds elapsed. Joe was stunned by her appearance.

He knew her. She was once his playmate and they had grown up in the same neighbourhood.

Her name was Jan Doe and Joe's recognition lifted him suddenly into an empathetic mode in which he knew that the calling had begun. With more vigour coupled with might, the men pushed the remaining sharp-edged metal that dangerously pointed at the victims.

The paramedics concurrently touched her and checked for a pulse, and found that it was stable, their hypothesis and conclusion sending them into heightened efforts of salvation.

Time passed slowly; in what seemed like an eternity, the workers managed to free Jan from the wreckage. She was coherent while being removed from the vehicle and was immediately rushed to the hospital.

Joe was filled with a peculiar tedium afterwards. For a while, the excitement was over. The job had been completed and it was *an experience that made him realize that this was just the beginning.*

It hit him when he was sitting home, pensively musing over the day's event. It was because Jan had been like a sister. He was greatly moved, groaning with much pain. He knew that it was unusual in one's first week at work to be found in a life-threatening situation in which a close friend was fatally involved.

Jan had died a few hours upon arrival. *She had a bright future and her death was a reminder to Joe that life was like wind that could be puffed away.* It gave him second thought about life and death. His grandparents would always remind him of the death and resurrection of *Jesus Christ,* and enunciated the importance of accepting him as *Lord and Saviour,* otherwise facing eternal damnation in hell. He prayed earnestly that Jan had confessed before meeting with her maker.

In her death, a courage like Everest rose to its apex within. He went all out that night, having being pushed to the limit, trying to save the life of someone that he had known all of his life.

The epoch to a dramatic, most daunting journey had been marked.

Story 12

An Act of Bravery

Joe was unfazed by the intimidation and mean spirited ways of his co-workers. *He wasn't surrounded entirely by haters. There were a few men that saw him for the man he was and not for his color.*

Even though he was crushed by most of their hurtful innuendo, he would not be found trailing back to the exit door.

There were times when Joe found objects placed in his bed. They ranged from bugs to toys and an array of sharp objects that were intended as jokes, but could have caused an injury or bodily harm to him. Joe truly believed that the Lord was protecting him from the traps meant to ensnare.

Many people within the area were going through much racial segregation; in fact, some had lost their lives in different parts of the country. It was an act of bravery, therefore; he stood in the midst of biased men, being the first black man to work in the department.

The tension as a result was like a furnace burning ten times the norm. He had accepted the possibility that his life could have been shortened by his co-workers, *but felt a profound sense of conviction to do what he was created to do, and that was to be a true fire-fighter.* Unlike before, when the toy truck was sandwiched between his fingers, swinging to and fro, reality had set in, and now the giant red fire engine towering above and around him was real, moving him towards the fulfilment of his calling.

Story 13

The Warehouse Fire

It was a quiet and still evening at No.1 Fire Station. *Suddenly,* the alarm sounded. It was a *three-alarm fire.* Within seconds, the station was empty. *Black smoke was visible; it was as if the entire city were ablaze.* Faithfully, the men rushed to stop the raging fire. It was an old warehouse fully engulfed that housed highly flammable materials and was furiously inflamed. The fire had spread to all parts of the building, the entrance enveloped in thick, black smoke. Fireman Joe quickly took the nozzle and went in first to quench the furious flames.

With no breathing apparatus, only protective gear, he felt the intense heat and smoke fighting the giant fire, as *David did when he fought Goliath.* Two other firemen were inside the warehouse with him, working as a team.

Duster began to feel the intense heat and smoke flooding his eyes. His breathing became erratic; seeking fresh air, Joe quickly decided to retreat, desperately trying to maintain his composure. He staggered through the thick, black smoke, the hose acting as a guide to the door. He couldn't breathe; the escape was mingled with a slow trot and emphatic gasping.

He was relieved to feel the edge of the door. But as quickly as he felt relief wash over him, so did panic; it settled hard and cold.

With perplexed realization and profound shock, he saw that the door to the warehouse was shut. Joe could not fathom how the escape route had been blocked; he searched blindly for another opening and became disoriented.

Death had curtained the passage of escape, insinuating treacherous intention. His cry for help yielded no results. The suspicion that it was the team on duty, who was now transformed into chameleons of loathing of his dark skin, left him enraged at the obvious, but gave him more reason to not give up and perish, giving his co-worker a morbid satisfaction. Evil wasn't supposed to triumph over good.

Joe felt as if it was not his time to perish; he pulled and tugged helplessly, his strength waning, ebbing away at every vehement effort of escape, slipping and escaping.

He descended toward the floor, desperate for life, his arms reaching at nothing for support, his death lingering, a foreboding feeling hovering all over. He landed on the floor, still fighting for breath, panting hopelessly.

Joe Duster's *heart raced, thudding against its walls;* his head pounded while the eyes took on a momentary glare. He could see his fingers shaking to a silent beat, as if moving to a mellow - blues number with a taunting title called "Fear."

Familiarity with fear always escaped him; their unsolicited meetings always felt virgin. Incoherent voices in the near distance resonated with protestations, and so thundered like a mighty fountain.

It was as if an army of - men clad in white had gathered. He was sure his fellow brothers outside had invited an insurgence. This villainous act suddenly triggered memories of Joe's childhood. The memories flooded before him like a film on a projector.

He succumbed and lost all consciousness....

The fluids spewed out of his mouth as oxygen permeated his lungs, and the hands that were pulling him up secured him from the thick, black warehouse smoke. He was lifted up by his hands and legs.

Joe was relieved that help had come; suddenly nostalgia engulfed him, Grandma's words recurring: "*God will supply you with all of your needs, and if you believe you will succeed.*" With frustration and anger, his eyes flooded. He didn't miss the irony of the situation, that the very men who had shackled him in the warehouse were his conduit to survival. He knew that there was a higher power at play, for many who had been privy to the cruelty of racial discrimination and its manifest criminality never had an opportunity to return and tell. He breathed in a sigh of thanks, giving, that to the One and only who watched over him in a time of need.

The men left him to recuperate as he regained his perceptions and coherence, wiping fluid off the sides of his mouth.

Joe felt a whirl of emotions, saddened that it was his brothers who had intended to undermine his existence.

There wasn't the Klan marching outside. It was due to delirium, making him hear a throng of voices while in the grip of death.

He went back to the firehouse dejected, fear hovering still.

Upon returning to the station, the same fire crew was sent out again on another call.

Story 14

Every Call was an Assignment

Nascent that day was a life of more betrayals and hurts. The days that ensued were encumbered with hefty workloads. His exhilaration did not wane on account of the judgmental stares that were an optical glare of hatred or the wagging tongues of detest; not even the audible sound of how the black man ought to have been swept off the American soil could deter his purpose.

He gallantly walked through the corridors that were a witness to his outward façade of bravery, and perhaps had even pulled off a sophisticated ploy of espionage to take a glimpse into that inner sanctum where he secured his most profound secret: his fear of failure.

Often, he thought the walls had ears and sometime would excite a discreet chuckle deep within. Joe always kept a smile on his face. It was during these times that he was in need of a bit of humour to survive the harsh racial terrain.

One day, interrupting one of his reclusive chats, the engine company was called to action. Joe had been around for a few years and was familiar with the drill. There was an accident and a human life was at stake.

The firemen on duty became busy, bustling with anxiety. Joe abhorred the thought that lay latent, threatening an impending death. He always attended to his case on duty with special attention. Every call was a mission of God's assignment on earth, and every loss of life he encountered during his duty left him tainted with profound remorse.

They had reached the area of the accident. The car was smashed badly; bystanders could clearly see that the car occupants were in much peril. Joe began to shift the equipment from the truck. He lumbered to the car, carrying the equipment alone, wondering where his fellow firemen were. His curious thought made him pass a probing eye around the vicinity.

They stood watching him as he took a quick inspection of the damaged vehicle; the men watched as he ducked his eyes from them and nipped back to the truck for more equipment. He was surprised to see them immobile and stagnant where he had left them.

Joe fathomed their ill intent. The three men trying to disrupt his calling stood as advocates of hate and refused to partner with him in fulfilling the mission.

As time would permit, he wasn't going to be dissuaded; as a lone soldier, he trotted from the truck, carrying equipment, and completed the salvage work alone. The men stood, watching him excel in his effort to save a life, effort that required much man power to achieve, and like vultures waiting for prey to weaken to then pounce on the prey, their sharp talons digging into flesh, the men stared with stone-cold eyes. Joe had been set up for failure, but with determination and the will of God, this was a mission accomplished.

Joe saved a life that day and went home feeling elated. A wide smile permeated from his heart to his face, affecting the world.

The walls of his bedroom witnessed his naked fears. That night, they saw a man downtrodden, shamefacedly yet inwardly lifted. He slept a deep sleep.

Story 15

Expected Failure

Joe now accepted the arrangement within the work schedule. He had become a rover and was floating around from one station to another. He was ready for a change. It meant that he was not assigned to one particular station.

During the summer of 1985, he was sent to Station #5 permanently. His enthusiasm really cascading, he was to report to a lieutenant he had been assigned to work with for the first time.

The ambience around was amicable. He asked for the lieutenant's office and was given direction by an off-duty fireman. The lieutenant was standing, facing the window. The day wasn't exactly sunny or warranting a spectator's keen watch, and the irony struck Joe that perhaps it was a time for a troubled man to reflect on his ills.

He turned his face, a silhouette against the ambient light, and Joe couldn't really pick out his features until he sat. The man had gentle eyes, revealing untold stories of many things that had happened. He could see that they were eyes that had known pain, and he sympathized somewhat.

Joe was greeted civilly, as was expected of a lieutenant to his junior, and he was later asked to take a seat. Then the man began a parody.

"I am going to teach you the ways of the white man and will break you like a stubborn stallion."

Joe understood quickly that he had misread the glare for gentleness. It represented a hateful man who stood hidden behind a guise. Joe wore a stoic demeanour but inside, as always, he was breaking—breaking because even though he had gotten himself inside, he was still being fought by the brothers he was supposed to be working hand in hand with to serve and protect. He felt disparaged a common feeling when his race was demeaned.

Having finished with the purpose of seeing the senior, Joe walked out of there feeling dejected, but the feeling of expected failure was more apparent.

Story 16

GOD'S Time

Time elapsed, unnoticed. He had so many things to do, so much to learn. There were many people to serve, save, and protect, many endangered animals to assist and to give his time to, which translated into life—a life he had given his nation.

One fine day, nothing seeming unusual in the beginning; he was finishing up his training and decided to take a shower to relax a little. The drops of water falling atop his head calmed him, as a soothing soda in a thirsty and dry oesophagus. His mind meandered over issues of the day, and purpose, as always, was considered. The showers that were taken were sometimes an opportunity to talk to God. Joe was in prayer.

Suddenly, arriving with a shock was the startling rush of cold water and ice being dumped over his head and body, sending him into an instant fright. The chilled water that had been poured for a long while undermined the hot water that poured through the shower head. The ice landed on the floor, shattering into pieces, and quickly his security fled. Searching to find what had just happened, he heard the sound of a metal pail quickly fading in the distance.

Someone had poured iced water over his head to send a message that he was still not wanted in the department.

It was then that he realized his heart had been jolted into an accelerated mode. Joe was *livid.* How could people hate so much?

He walked out of the shower, asking the very question, when he met a fellow fire-fighter. Immediately his mouth erupted into gleeful splendour, feeling the joy of passing regards to another human being. *He loved people and no amount of cold intimidation was going to trample on what his Maker had given him.*

3

Story 17

History Repeating Itself

It was November and the thrills that come with the season were apparent. Everyone seemed to be high-spirited at the station that Thursday afternoon. The ambience was enchanting, charming, and Joe, too, was captivated by the spell.

It was in between a jest and a jeer from a group of fire-fighters that he exited the building to go to his car briefly. He dashed to the parked car and, within seconds, the sight that caught his eye made his heart sink.

THE FIRE TRUCKS WERE LEAVING THE STATION.
Joe did not hear the alarm. He realized the implications of failing to respond and the ineptness of not doing so bruised his ego. *It was impossible to hear the alert tone with the doors down.*

On impulse, Joe emptied his hands and begun sprinting vigorously, animated by his failure. He ran fast in pursuit of the departing trucks, his virile agility acting as the impetus impelling him forward. His desperation forced him into further pursuit, but the driver of the truck ahead of him, seeing Duster in the side mirror, stepped on the accelerator and the truck veered onto the next street, broadening the gap between man and machine.

His feet's velocity slowed with the truck's speedy departure. He stood and watched the truck disappear on the horizon. He tried to act composed, swallowing hard at nothing. He stood looking at the empty streets for an instant, still trying to digest what had just transpired. He walked back to the station, defeated.

As with fear, he couldn't bring himself to befriend racism. Joe sat in the parking lot dispiritedly, gloomily musing.

The following weeks, he was given one shift off, without pay, and one-year probation.

Months passed amid racial tension at work, but Joe had long decided that since the warehouse incident, he would not let any man, of whatever creed or color, intimidate him further. He would rather have died than give them the satisfaction of quitting.

He had been assigned to Station #3, working as a fire-fighter, and the lieutenant was absent so the assigned driver of the fire apparatus was moved up to lieutenant-trainee and Joe was supposedly moved to driver-trainee. Another man was sent to take his assignment as a fire-fighter.

The department had a chain of command. Headquarters was also known as Station #1, while the rest of the stations were called "out-stations" because they were manned twenty-four/seven in another district. There were four fire stations in the city at the time, with three men per out-station. At Station #5, there were five men because it housed two engine companies.

Headquarters accommodated several ranking officers, ranging from a battalion chief, captains, lieutenants and engineers. An Engineer in the fire service is commonly known as the driver of a fire apparatus. Extra men would be sent out when a fire-fighter was off at another Station.

The lieutenant assigned to Station #3 was off and the lower-ranking fire-fighter would replace the immediate higher-ranking officer.

The captain approached the engineer and asked him to step into the shoes of the unavailable lieutenant, as acting lieutenant but to still keep his position as driver because, as time would have it, Joe was next in line to be a driver. The engineer refused and adamantly insisted he would not be taking two positions at once. He said to the captain, "*What about Joe?*" The captain, who hadn't anticipated the engineer to have an inclination towards Joe, succumbed.

For Joe, that day was highly momentous and he was hopeful it would be the beginning of even better days in the service. He knew the captain wasn't happy to see him sitting in the driver's seat of the fire truck, checking its gears and inspecting machinery, as a delighted novice would, but now he was a man who had endured the fire of racial discrimination and stood refined as a bar of fine gold.

That very day, Joe started training as a driver at Fire Station #3 and it was because of one man, an engineer, who stood up for what he truly thought was right. This man chose to see Joe for who he was instead of the color that he was.

Having worked under three fire chiefs, years elapsed and Joe had survived the times. He had seen men join the service and leave, and he knew his portion was to hang on for a longer while.

He had earned a modicum of respect among a few friends, and a few black men had joined the department. The barrage of insinuations and blatant racism never stopped, although it abated somewhat after a 260 pound Battalion Chief jumped on his back while eating supper and the years that had passed was making Joe become a hard man. He had learned to cope with his reality and, in all this, change in him was apparent, unavoidable. He didn't realize himself the damage from the events in the military, coupled with the exposure of injustice had done to him. He simply thought he had mastered the coping mechanisms of pain and hatred.

In the summer of 1993, during one of the many expeditions he had been on, Joe obtained an injury. It happened swiftly; he didn't see it coming and hid his anxiety from his co-workers by constantly repeating that he was going to be just fine. The repercussions that came were an impediment that affected him.

The injury happened while exiting a fire engine. He was perturbed by his accident and prayed to God that He would restore him quickly, so that he would return to his job. Fire fighting was his life and he needed to exist as one functioning actively.

One Friday afternoon during his absence, he received a phone call from the chief's office. He left home with a feeling of uneasiness, fearing a letter of termination because of his injury. Instead, he was welcomed by a pleasant surprise. His leg still wrapped in plaster of Paris, and with a slight limp, he was met by the fire chief. "Congratulations," history had again repeated itself he said. "You have been promoted." It was with a sigh of relief that Joe was the first black man to become a high ranking officer, *Lieutenant/Fire Inspector.*

Although highly exhilarated, Joe was a man who always hid his emotions and never made a dramatic display of them. Being calm as usual, he received the promotion and returned to work serving in the new position.

He was a strong, middle-aged man, but the leg kept failing him and the visit to the doctor came with a recommendation for two more surgeries. The doctor advised that he should not exert much pressure on the injury, and sent him back to work on light duty.

He was keen to return, even if it meant only relegated to a desk job, but much to his disappointment, he quickly learned that there was no provision for relaxed terms in the fire service at the time. There was no light duty.

Joe retired early on grounds of disability. His career ended suddenly without him preparing adequately for a departure from his passion, his realized dream. He felt the drying of a tender part once more. Pain was always surfacing, transforming the gentle into a coarse disposition.

Story 18

The Beginning of a Hardened Heart

He settled at home indifferently, hoping to heal from the pain because of his early retirement, with nowhere to turn and not knowing if anyone would understand. His energetic spirit felt the need to be out in the world, catering to the public. He missed his work with a threatening passion. It was as if he would become unglued.

Joe was hurting. *He profoundly missed being a fire-fighter. He felt fear creeping upon him, as it sometimes did during his childhood.*

Standing as titans of might, the little shreds of dignity he had was mashed into nothingness.

He had an abundance of free time on his hands, ushering with it the opportunity to reflect on and ponder life's calamities. He started seeing a woman but he didn't really fathom her. She had become an enigma to him. He didn't like the need he felt for her; it was the power she brandished before him, a taunting strength that evaporated him that he sometimes detested. It was this very power that emerged strong, allowing him to fall for her, yet he despised her strength, ironically feeling a very strong need to be with her, a need to be loved by her, held, and acknowledged by her.

He did realize that this need for affection from her was deeply rooted from birth, having been told by his grandma how his mother attempted to abort her pregnancy and, the hand of the Lord too strong, Grandma was close by to receive him to safety and therefore raised him. He needed a woman to close the gap that had been widened throughout his life.

Joe dated many women in the search for true love. This man simply wanted and needed to be loved, and in return give the love that was housed inside, *thinking perhaps his secret desperations would be over if he found the right woman. She would be expected to fill the enormous responsibility of replicating the love unfulfilled in his pain-fraught life.*

Then came the post-mortem on his work and the relationship he had with his colleagues. A pain indefinable rested dormant. There was indeed an implosion within him and the years in the fire service, being segregated, had changed the *soft young man into a **selfish man**.*

Presented with the reality of the loss of a job that he truly loved, he turned those who surrounded him into victims of his anger for his unrequited love and broken dreams. ***He was an angry man. It was the beginning of a HARDENED HEART.***

⸺⊷⊶⊷⸺

From 1979 to 1997 she had been there, always, as a loving and noble wife. Her name was Katina. Encouraging him to work hard during his journey through the academy, she made sure that Joe had quiet moments to study and was always the human reminder of his time. He appreciated her efforts to make him a better, educated man and foresaw a long future with Katina. However, in the depravity of moral fibre, it being stained with selfishness, he began to cheat on his wife.

He never wanted to hurt her but felt the urgency to move on, desperately searching to find the love that was needed as a child, the love that his mother had denied him. Joe began a reckless quest for unfound love; the woman who had become his best friend and encourager was now hurting from his acts of infidelity. Joe was consumed by the search, not caring whose heart he had crushed. He acknowledged Katina's hurts, but cast an unseeing eye to her pain—everything suddenly was about him. His needs, losses, pain, and betrayals. This man was crying out for someone to understand, someone to help him find the missing part of his life. Upon being served with divorce papers, his pain struck once again. He would remain with deep respect and benign memories of her forever.

Having been married for years, and having a daughter he adored and loved so dearly, Joe was sure that his first child would fill the void that kept eating at him. Even the name that he had given her meant so much: Chandelis. Chan: meaning cute. Delis: meaning pleasure, delight. She embodied all the love that he needed from his mother, and in her childish mollification, he knew that she gave him all her heart's love without reservation. Her presence always brought the light to darkness and he always felt calm, in her presence.

But it wasn't enough to free him from the pain that was embedded inside. It was more than this man could handle in this natural world.

It was during this desperate moment in time that he lost touch with his spirituality and innate self. The relationship he had with his Saviour had tumbled and, being self-absorbed, he felt everything was as intended by nature. He stopped having the private moments of meditation and spent less time reading the Bible. Joe interpreted all this as a phase in his life and continued the search for his much-needed satisfaction, validation in life, and to meet the need of recognition. *He knew there was a God somewhere, and inwardly he acknowledged the separation between them, but the lack of inner strength was wheeling him further away, turning him into a degenerate, rancorous being.*

Even though he managed to conceal much of his hurt behind the smile that he wore, the unpleasantness, like an uncontrollable virus, had spread further from home and a few others had started noticing the transformation.

There was a trip sponsored by *a Christian organization to* Washington, D.C. via Florence, Alabama, eager to *stand up for the Lord,* evangelize, and spread the *Good News of the Gospel.* Shamelessly, Joe didn't attend. ***HE DID NOT STAND UP FOR THE LORD.***

With the villainy exposed, manifestly at work, he felt a reckless abandon of self and was swept by the wild currents of his whims. In the process, everything crumbled before his very eyes and he lost the partnership he had in marriage. He had stained the sanctity of his bed, soiled the trust she had for him. He had done to her the very thing he had been fighting against. It was if he had become the monster he had spent his whole life trying not to be.

His marriage ended. At this point Joe cared less about himself, recognizing the vile man he had become by destroying the love that stood true around him. Despite all the pandemonium in his life, his hope and love for his daughter remained unshaken and unthreatened. Joe's love for *Chandelis* stood firm, grounded, and soaring.

A loss of God in his life, his friends death in San Diego, the premature departure from his job, and everything crumbling around him suddenly evoked memories and brought out the child in him as he sought for his *heart's* persuasions, heightening the emotional stress.

Story 19

The Helms of Death

Joe Duster was fortunate in his lifetime, despite *his departure from the fire service, to have saved eight individuals from the helms of death,* both children and adults. These experiences gave him the satisfaction he had been longing for, and that was to save lives. *There are three events that stood out the most: they involved an infant and two small children.*

Late one hot summer, Joe had recently returned from the military and was taking an evening stroll when he heard women and children crying and screaming. The family was horrified. Without thinking, he ran in to assist. It was a very small infant that had been lifted from its crib. It was strange that Joe had been reading an article about crib death.

Having received first aid and CPR training in the Navy, Joe asked the mother to give him the infant. The mother was frantic and did not refuse. Checking his pulse and breathing, he found no sign of life. The infant had turned blue and was not breathing. *Joe stuck his fingers inside the infant's mouth, and began removing clabbered milk, which had clogged the child's airway.* Joe beckoned for his friend Frank, who was coasting by, shouting in a high-pitched voice for him to stop. The car came to a screeching halt, Joe jumped in, and the car sped off with him and the infant.

En route to the hospital, Joe was performing CPR. *Upon arrival, the infant began to cry;* it was the baby's beginning of a new life.

One rainy afternoon while sitting on his Cousin Jean's front porch enjoying the cool afternoon, suddenly without warning there stood Jean in tears with her son in her arms. He was limp, his eyes closed and a shallow pulse; his life was slipping away. *The young lad had stopped breathing.* Joe administered CPR to the ailing young boy as time slipped away.

Luckily a policeman, that was patrolling the area, stopped and offered his assistance. With the baby in his arms, Joe quickly entered the back seat of the vehicle. The officer immediately left the scene in a professional manner and in route to the hospital the young lad regained consciousness. The child was later released from the hospital in good condition.

It was a weekend in which family and friends gathered at the Dusters' home for a friendly game of cards; his daughter was playing with her cousins as usual. *Chandelis was three years old at the time* when it was brought to his attention that she was in a precarious situation.

He was quickly led to an *airtight suit case in which his daughter was encased;* the suitcase was outdated and *locked, with no key.* It lay on the floor; shocking knowledge brought feverish fear on him with an impact. Chandelis's life was hanging on the brink of survival and Joe instinctively fought to free her from the suitcase.

He knew that her oxygen supply was limited and seconds had ticked by, lessening the chances of her being found alive. Worried that his daughter wasn't alive, he called incessantly and probed for a response. *Hearing her voice, a very faint sound as in a distance.* Joe expressed his desperate love for his daughter that day by fighting with the airtight suitcase, using only his bare hands; his fatherly instincts kicking in aggressively, beads of sweat spread out on the smooth plane of his forehead.

The suitcase snapped in his hands as he forwarded the core strength of his very life, fearing for the little person that had more of a reason and need to see tomorrow.

He held her in a tight embrace, relief resting upon him, her tiny body warm to the touch. *She meant the world to him.*

Story 20

The Other Side

Months had passed; his divorce was final. Joe's mother became terminally ill and was admitted to the hospital. He and his brother Andrew felt a strong need to pray with and for the patients in the *west wing,* encouraging ones with tender hearts and feeble minds to be strong.

Through the years, Joe had been diligently seeking a stronger relationship with Jesus Christ; he was seeking righteousness.

On the penultimate day before her passing, *the clock in Mary's room had stopped.* Concurrently, the man whom Joe had said a prayer for across the hall passed away. After this, Joe decided to frequently visit the hospital, hoping, in spite of all that he hadn't shared with his mother as a son, that perhaps something would be mended. She was his mother and he was going to give her the respect that she deserved in her last moments on earth because, in spite of it all, she was the vehicle God had used to transport him to earth.

The day was as usual. If it wasn't for the foreboding feeling he had, he would have called it a perfect day.

When Joe entered her room, a very unusual event was occurring. Her perception bleary, *she was having a conversation with her deceased family members, calling each one by name.* He made no attempt to intervene and politely sat beside her bed.

Time began to pass slowly; she looked at her son and began to speak, slowly and uninterrupted. She said, *"I am tired."* After a long pause, Mary Louise spoke again. *"I am ready to go home."*

The very last words that Joe and his sister Pam heard their mother say were, "*I am sorry.*"

The words she spoke lingered in his mind as he looked on piteously at a life that had hurt him so much. *She died peacefully while he stood looking on solemnly.*

He felt numb and had not grasped the meaning of what she had meant with the last statements. He knew her as a stoic woman, one who hardly revealed any form of emotion towards him. *However, the words she had spoken signified a heart capable of having experienced the paradigms of love.*

He sought *the Lord in prayer,* asking what she could have meant, and by *divine understanding,* it was as stated: *She was tired of suffering in this world, she was ready to go and be with the Lord Jesus. She was truly sorry that he wasn't going with her to the other side.*

The insight gave him a sense of peace with his mother and this was from deducing that she had a relationship with her Maker before entering the transitory passage to meet him. Joe loved his mother and he knew that she loved him even more.

Story 21

A Command with Complete Authority

Joe's mother was laid to rest on the twenty-seventh day of December 2003. Seven days after she had been buried, Joe was asleep in his **bedroom when he was awakened by a shrewd tug on his shoulder.** When he turned to acknowledge it, he was met by a *beast* with three heads, connected to a *dragon, with the tail of a serpent.* It was a dirty, greyish color and beheld him with imploring red eyes and legs like a lion. It made an eerie sound that he had never heard before. It looked to be a thousand years old whilst its smell reminded him of a dead fish.

Joe scampered from the bedroom in a frightful frenzy, fear consuming his very being. He could feel himself shivering within, *a part of him wishing it was just a dream; but it was not.* Everything that had happened was real; reality had begun the moment he was awakened.

This wasn't a premonition, a vision, or a dream.

His heart was beating much faster than normal; fear had flashed its canines. Joe was overwhelmed. He returned to his room while still in the valley of indecision. Hoping that perhaps it could have been a mere dream, it seemed as if everything began to curtail as he took baby steps while entering the room. He had always met intimidation clad in a suit with a taunting designer-label marked "fear." *But not like this.* His life at that point was a mockery. He was so overwhelmed with trepidation it took time for him to re-enter his bedroom, and once inside, he was exorbitantly relieved to see that the creature had vanished.

Joe rushed to the bedside and began to pray like never before. It seemed as if his mind had been altered. *The experience of seeing the creature was horrifying, the fear unbearable. He was praying for the*

Lord to free him from being consumed by the terrible dragon or remove him from this earth. He was still sweating profusely. It was unbearable.

Without warning, there was a bright light that shone in the bedroom and settled, illuminating. *The light was brighter than anything he had ever encountered but it wasn't disturbing or blinding to the eye.* All manner of comprehension left him, escaping his intellectual faculties. The events unfolding didn't seem real.

As Joe continued *crying for the Lord to take him* and free him from the troubles of this natural world, ***suddenly a voice with the mighty sound of rushing water, ten thousand times louder than a sonic boom, incomprehensive to the human mind, spoke. And it said,***
"IF YOU DON'T STAND UP FOR ME, WHY SHOULD I STAND UP FOR YOU?"

Joe's life was being exposed it was happening so fast that he could not grasp *anything.*

There was one thing for sure: Joe Louis Duster knew that it was an encounter with the ***HOLY SPIRIT.***

Joe continued praying timidly; *then the voice spoke again, at once, and gave him a command.* ***WITH COMPLETE AUTHORITY,*** *it said*:

> ***"YOU SPREAD THESE WORDS. LET NOT YOUR HEART***
> ***BE HARDENED FOR THE THINGS OF***
> ***THIS WORLD; MY WORDS ARE TRUE, PURE, AND***
> ***EVERLASTING…ALL THINGS OF***
> ***THIS WORLD SHALL COME TO PASS."***

Joe Louis Duster, 2004

Suddenly, Joe was at *peace;* everything returned to normal. He felt a sense of tranquillity engulf his surroundings. Moving slowly, as if exiting a trance, and sweating profusely, he quietly shut his bedroom door, tottering to the living quarters to behold the sky and *worshiping with thanksgiving* to the *Lord* for having saved him from the *BEAST*.

His outlook on life had been changed; the *Almighty* had given him a second chance. He could have been taken by Asmodeus or Asmodai from The Book of Tobit (Book of Tobias), the King of demons, the father of monsters. Asmodeus is the demon that inspires gambling, deceit, lust and revenge. He had come for Joe's soul. It is said that people who fall to Asmodeus' ways will be sentenced to an eternity in the *second level of hell.* "This man knew that if his physical life had ended, his destination would have been *hell.*"

For the first time in his life, Joe experienced peace. It was from that momentous time that he derived an interest in truly knowing the Lord and questioned the efficacy of his past relationship. It was then that he became truly born again. He began to read the Bible keenly and pray earnestly, as he had never done before. Having been raised by God-fearing relatives, and with the thought of being born again, he felt the eventful night with the creature spelt a rebirth in his relationship with the Lord.

From then on, Joe decided to rededicate the rest of his life to spreading the word of God in whatever form of media available. He felt as if burdensome scales that had encased him were suddenly removed by the Lord. A new man was born indeed. It was in this period of recognizance that he felt wholeness within. God heard his cry.

He felt for the first time that the Lord loved him enough to suffice for the love he didn't get from his mother or any other woman in this natural world. He didn't need to be loved by a woman to feel wanted, or have a woman masquerading as his mother for him to feel whole. Jesus resided within him; therefore, it would be no love lost. Jesus is love Himself!

As an eventual revelation dawned that it was only in the Lord Jesus Christ that he was made complete, and his desperate quest for love was now forever over, his heart rested and truly settled.

EPILOGUE

JOE LOUIS DUSTER lives to spread the Gospel of Jesus Christ in unconventional ways, enunciating with clarion clarity.

"ALL THINGS THAT ARE ACCOMPLISHED AND ACQUIRED BY YOU IN RIGHTEOUSNESS SHOULD BE PASSED ON... OR YOU HAVE LIVED YOUR LIFE IN VAIN."

Joe Louis Duster, 2004

Mr. Duster's assignment from the Almighty God escalated from saving lives and property to savings souls. Joe now offers consultancy in fire protection/fire safety and will spend the rest of his life seeking Righteousness, sharing the True Love of God. *He is a witness that Jesus Christ is the TRUE LIGHT of this world.*

HEBREW 3:12-15: *"Beware then of your own hearts, dear brothers, lest you find that they, too, are evil and unbelieving and are leading you away from the living God. Speak to each other about these things every day while there is still time, so that none of you will become hardened against God, being blinded by the glamour of sin. For if we are faithful to the end, trusting God just as we did when we first became Christians, we will share in all that belongs to Christ.*

"But now is the time. Never forget the warning, 'Today if you hear God's voice speaking to you, do not harden your hearts against him, as the people of Israel did when they rebelled against him in the desert'" (The Living Bible, paraphrased).

AUTHOR'S NOTE

FIRST AND FOREMOST, I give all adoration, praise, and honour to the Almighty God, Jesus Christ, my Lord and Saviour. I bear witness to the miraculous power of the Holy Spirit. Words cannot describe the things that I felt while sharing and writing a story about my life.

At first I was reluctant because I knew that it would be a very challenging project. But God intervened and placed three people in my life that encouraged me through the most crucial times of my life. Joe Beck, Santonia (Nanny) Johnson, and Eddie Summerhill inspired me to publish this book. They gave me the initiative to succeed and understood the struggles and hardships that were placed in front of me, which encouraged me to excel. Nanny and my grandmother Hattie Mae would always tell me, God will supply you with all of your needs and if you believe, you will succeed.

There are approximately 1.7 million people in the city of Lusaka, Zambia, the southern part of Africa, and the Almighty God took me there in Spirit and allowed me to share my testimony with a profound writer, who would have a significant impact on my life. *I am without a doubt that this book is a true testament. It proves that there is no limitation on how far the Holy Spirit can travel, and whom it is capable of traveling through.*

I was, again hesitant about sharing my life story with someone that I'd never met before. But the innermost part of me proclaimed peace, therefore bypassing the natural entering into the Spirit Realm. Since the beginning of time, man has underestimated the power of the True, Living God and continues to do so as of this day. The discovery of the Internet is allowing His word to be distributed more efficiently and effectively in this modern day and time. We live in a very fast-paced society and people have become lovers of themselves. It is "I" and "my" instead of "us" and "we." The innocent are prosecuted while the guilty go free.

There are so many things in this world that can cause one's heart to become hardened: jealousy, envy, hatred, the love that one has for money, power, and flesh. There is a greater need for more patience, kindness, love, peace, faith, and forgiveness. "The same God that spoke yesterday, still speaks today, and is the same God that will speak tomorrow and forever."

When we all stand before the judgment seat of God, He is not going to ask you what it is that you have done that makes you worthy of entering the gates of Heaven. He is going to ask you, "What have you done for others?"

Muya Monique Nkazi, I cannot thank you enough for believing in me.

My prayer is that God will allow the United States of America and Zambia, the southern part Africa; forever, build bridges of peace, love, and harmony.

Joe Louis Duster

ROMANS 14:7-12: "We are not our own bosses to live or die as we ourselves might choose. Living or dying we follow the Lord. Either way we are his. Christ died and rose again for this very purpose, so that he can be our Lord both while we live and when we die. You have no right to criticize your brother or look down on him. Remember, each of us will stand personally before the Judgment Seat of God. For it is written, 'As I live,' says the Lord, 'every knee shall bow to me and every tongue confess to God.' Yes, each of us will give an account of himself to God" (*The Living Bible, paraphrased*).

MATTHEW 24:13-14: "But those enduring to the end shall be saved. And the Good News about the Kingdom will be preached throughout the whole world, so that all nations will hear it, and then, finally, the end will come" (*The Living Bible, paraphrased*).

"LET NOT YOUR HEART BE HARDENED"

WRITER'S NOTE

THERE ISN'T A single word that can express the *emotional journey* that I experienced whilst writing the biography of Mr. Joe Louis Duster, and so I attempt to concise everything in a few words.

When Mr. Duster suggested that he and I write a story of his life, I wasn't sure if I could arise to his expectations satisfactorily. Although *I did encourage myself in the Scripture that says, "I can do all things through Christ who strengthens me,"* I was an unpublished writer and I sometime felt as if I was undertaking a project that was beyond me. The thought of writing a rich history of a retired, celebrated lieutenant/fire inspector was very intimidating, but I braved the cause because it was an honorable challenge.

It wasn't easy writing the story because Mr. Duster and I have never met before. *So I had to collect the historical data over the Internet and telephone.* I therefore struggled with accuracy of data sometimes and had to revert to consultation.

The peculiar single thing that stood out was the way I felt when writing some emotional scenes. I used to feel like I was going through the very situation he had been through and so found it easy to write the narrative.

I enjoyed writing the manuscript because of the triangulated emotional journey. It is as if the story was set to have a flow that was easy for me to tap in to.

Having finished, I now feel that I've triumphed a test and have attained the hidden advantage of my achievements. It was an honor to have worked with Mr. Duster on this project. It is also an even greater honor and privilege to have been asked to write as an African writer. I cannot say "thank you" enough for the confidence, Mr. Duster that you had in me.

This book is a true testament of how distance can be bridged by the pen as the United States of America and Zambia, the southern part of Africa, unite on realms on paper.

We would like to say thank you Mr. Joe Duster for giving us a privilege to come in contact with the vast story of your life. We acknowledge the pains that you encountered of both a challenged childhood and a lifetime fraught with racism.

You lumbered, suffered and put your own life in peril and in spite of all the obstacles you faced, you emerged a victor, the value of your own life relegated.

As a people who went through colonialism and had to sacrifice our people's blood for freedom, we understand your eventful journey, in our eyes, you are sort of Kaunda, a Mandela for setting the pace for others to come and freely enjoy your suffering.

Today we know many are living the American dream of emancipation in an Alabama Fire Department because of your selfless sacrifice in the fire service. Zambia the southern part of Africa recognizes and we hope that the state of Alabama one day will too.

Muya Monique Nkazi

.